Unspoken Words

(of Unheard of Thoughts)

by

Devlynn E. Javon

DORRANCE
PUBLISHING CO
EST. 1920
PITTSBURGH, PENNSYLVANIA 15238

Dorrance Publishing Co
585 Alpha Drive
Suite 103
Pittsburgh, PA 15238
Visit our website at *www.dorrancebookstore.com*

ISBN: 978-1-4809-5536-3
eISBN: 978-1-4809-5559-2

This Book

This book is me,
This is my heart
This is my soul
Every question
People want to know
Every night
As I stay up and think
I grab a pen
And waste not
It's ink.

The Mind

A golden tongue
Needs a golden brain
For with a tainted cerebrum
The gold will change
A man known for wisdom
Is born a fool
A man known to hate
Has lost his love
Or hasn't experienced
What he is capable of
Understand to listen
Not to speak
The difference between cowards
The weak
And meek

Simple

As simple as it sounds
We trust the man
Who looks us in our eyes
And tells a lie
As simple as it sounds
We feed the man
Who feeds himself
And not the town
As simple as it sounds
We give life to the man
Who's about to die
As simple as it sounds
We bring pain
To those
About to cry
As simple as it sounds
We cut wings to those
About to fly
As simple as it sounds
I ask questions
Yet I know why
As simple as it sounds
Let me live
And let me fly

The Past

Every day isn't promised
Every promise isn't kept
I remember when house was filled with sunshine
Now the sun has overslept,
When time was of the essence
And we learned from every lesson
We respected one another
And had love from our brothers
Now we lie, steal, and cheat
And dishonor our mothers
I remember kids used to play
Now they sleep
Depressed all day
And every promise
We chose to keep
Nowadays
We just don't think
And as for death
We would always weep
for another life
We pray to see

The Dream

I went for a ride on a Pegasus
I went for a ride in a dream
I saw birds swim
Fish fly and
Grass forever green
We dodged rain
Watched it pass us,
Indulged in wine
From exquisite glasses
Fed dragons
Fought ogres
Also saved the world
From being over
Once I woke
Saw the sun
While in the dream no more
I stepped out of bed and there she was
The Pegasus at the door.

A Friend

Tell me your problems
And I will listen
Tell me your pain
And I will fix it
If you're drowning
I will dive
If you are falling
I will fly
In open arms you will fall
For taking on a world so strong
In open arms
I will receive you
Trust and believe
I'll never deceive you
Show me your pain
And I will take it
Show me love and
we will make it
And if a life
Is not mine to take
Pray another life
I will make

Woman

She can debouch a man
With one look in his eyes
She carried breakfast, lunch, and dinner
All between her thighs
Never showed a weakness
She only showed her muscle
Didn't shy away from problems
To every man she showed her hustle
The way she speaks
I indulge in every expression
The way she rocks her body
Lord knows that she's a blessing

Queen

Beauty doesn't describe her
She's a gift far greater than that
The way she smiles
Turns,
And looks back
The way she speaks
Such a beautiful tone
She has it all
And did on her own
She was something
That I failed to keep
Strengthened my soul
While making me weak
My every thought
When I failed to speak

Lost

Lost in a world
That doesn't love itself
Lost in a world
That only loves its wealth
Sometimes I feel lost
Which makes me ponder
Makes me pause
Sit back and wonder
Will I ever find myself?
Or continue the traditions
To try and find my own wealth
Will I be lost
Every single day
or will someone help me
As I find my way?

?

What is life
What is death
What is left
Inside my chest
What is given
What was took
What are the words
Inside this book
What was seen
What was told
What makes us weak
What makes us bold
What's in the sky
How can I fly
What makes us wonder
What makes us cry
What makes us late
What makes us trust
What makes us do it
Just because
But most of all
What makes us love

Street Clothes

He had a stern face
And an old soul
He had plenty of jokes
And a heart not cold
Look at him walk
In his street clothes
Never had it all
But he never had nothing
His character gentle
And his voice was something
Like a kid in a shelter
He only wanted one thing
Look at him walk
In his street clothes
As he grew
He understood life
He knew in his heart
The wrong from right
As he grew
He continued to unfold
He steadily grew wise
He quickly grew old
Look at him walk
In his street clothes

Cloudy Days

I gave up on happiness
And accepting pain
I gave up on sunshine
In return for rain
Because these things
I am used to
These are the things
That a young boy knew
But don't give up on me
And I won't give up on you
Wait receive me
And always stay true

Addictions

I'm addicted to alcohol and sleep
I don't need love
That you can keep
There were times
I was drowning
In my own depression
Searching for attention
While hiding expression
These times are now over, however
Because I simply gave up
I live not to succeed
But to only see
That others won't choose
The same path as me
The road that leads
To misery
If I can make them smile
If I can bring them joy
I will do all that I can
This is my only choice

To Dad

Okay, Pops
I see you high
Okay, Pops
I wonder why
In this world
I am your seed
In this world
Alone to be
To teach myself
That which is true
To teach myself
Not to hate you
I teach myself
To be a man
To have faith
And do all I can
You left me at only five
You left me
And it blew my mind
These things in life
I had to teach myself
To put my problems
Up on the shelf
These problems in life
I do not know
Why'd you leave me
In this world alone
Ok pops I see you high
Ok pops I wonder why

Run Away

Yeah, I used to run away
To a place far, far away
Where people flew
Instead of planes
There was no more sorrow
No more pain
I ran away a thousand times
To a place that was only mine
In this place you don't have to listen
You don't have to be shy or distant
You don't have to hustle, drink, or smoke
C'mon, let's run 'til we can't run no more
Now that I'm older
I run no more
There's no place with an open door
I wish I can run back in time
Run away
To the special place in my mind

Wonder

I wanna be an artist
Or maybe a musician
I can paint a piano
Play the notes
And everyone will listen
I wanna change the world
They can call me a hero
I can end world hunger
And fight against evil
So many things in this world
That I seek to be
But at the end of the day
All I can be is me
And if I lose sight
Of that which is true
Please stand to correct me
And teach one what to do

Beauty

Her looks are so memorizing
Her lips are so sweet
A tingle they have when she looks at me
A heart so soft
With the touch of pain
A pattern over and over
And over of being hurt again
How brown her skin
How precious her love
I once held her heart
But now it's moved on
And torn mine apart

Life

Life breaks us down
So we can build ourselves up
Life humbles us
So we don't need to act tough
Life will keep going
When we think we've had enough
Life gives us hate
So we can understand love
Life knocks us down
So we can learn to get up
Life is complicated
And at times a little rough
Life can be a test, this I know
So when you think about stopping
Don't

Jail

I need a home-cooked meal
And a shower that's hot
I need a full-size bed
And sex
Whether she loves me
or loves me not
Fuck a phone call
I wanna talk face to face
I need to see the sun
Instead of this room, where I poll
I need to talk to the girl
Who has freckles and smiles
Or that one chick from Dallas
Who I haven't seen in a while
I need to call my people up
And tell them let's smoke
I need to sit in a room
Be the center of all jokes
I need to have a bottle of water
In which the bottle's clear
But most of all
I need to get
The fuck up out of here

Depression

Sometimes I wanna live
Sometimes I wanna fly
Sometimes I wanna try
Sometimes I was fun
But in the end
Sometimes I wanna die
Sometimes I wanna grow
Sometimes I wanna fold
Sometimes I wanna explode
Sometimes I'm feeling low
But there is given
Sometimes I wanna die
Sometimes I want a brother
Sometimes I want a mother
Sometimes I want a sister
Sometimes I want a father
But most of all
Sometimes I wanna die
Sometimes I wanna win
Sometimes I wanna give
Sometimes I wanna to live
Then I remember
Sometimes I wanna die

Shattered

I break like glass
To the world I'm hard as steel
Dying to live
So I must live to kill
All chances taken
Every dream's awakened
Who am I to be
Who are they to see
What's in my heart
What's real to me
And for the truth
That I will not find
Because I keep scrolling
As I'm stuck in rewind
I keep on going
I will not break
This is a chance
I have to take

Until Then

'til death do us both part
'til love mends broken hearts
Let the ground break and shake the sky
For I will hate and know not why
Taken from this world so soon
Patiently waiting for your petals to bloom
You tell me be strong
But I am only a man
You tell me to love and do all I can
Why is it the good ones go so young
Leaving a life that barely began
I have faith to see you again
A mother, a daughter, a true best friend
So as you live beyond the light
"I love you" is all that sounds right
So until death do us both apart
You will always live within our hearts

Help

Is it angels or demons
I can't really see
My vision is clouded by this life
And it's really messing with me
I can't leave it alone
Because in this world
I am alone
God, tell me
Am I
Who I'm really
Meant to be

Secret to My Success

The secret to my success
Is not due to the fact that I was rich
The secret to my success
Is not due to my patience
The secret of my success
Is not due to my religion, or
The fact that others lifted me up
Or put me to shame
The secret to my success
is due to the fact
That at once
I saw success
In my failure

You

My life has brought me misery
And misery loves company
but it'll have to do
Without me
And Mama
When I die be not dismayed
Don't mourn my demise
For you too will fly one day
No matter if
I'm loved by many
Or loved by few
Just know
I'll always love
You

Love

Sharper than the sharpest sword
It pierced my heart and made it sore
Never to be fixed
Or healed again
It is magic
Not made by man
When it lasts
It lasts for eternity
But love came
And left its burn on me
Never to be fixed or
Healed again
Curse this curse
Not made by man

Betrayed

When I wanna look at you
You look away
When I wanna hear you
You speak the other way
When I yearn to hold you
You push me away
This is why
I am who I am
No more a child
And more than a man
There are reasons why
I deny love
And reasons
Why I accept pain
Cuz if love was real
It would never end

Reality

At night I sleep
Holding my pillow
Wishing it was you
at night I sleep
Not believing
What we shared was through
Realizing the dreams, I had
Will never become true
At night I sleep
Realizing that you've had enough
Realizing everything we had
Was way beyond lost
At night I sleep
And in my dreams, you I come across
At night I sleep alone
 Because you were the best thing I let
And when I wake and pray to God
I pray you find the one
Who will give you his all

Deserve

Do I deserve this life I live
Life of treachery
Life of greed
Do I deserve this life I live?
I have nothing
But yet I give
Do I deserve this breath I breathe
My smile shows
But yet I grieve
Do I serve the one I love?
There's no one close
No one to hug
Do I deserve a helping hand?
Do I own the right to be a man?
Do I deserve what others don't have?
If not
I'll give all I can
Do I deserve this life I lead?
Life of treachery
Life of greed
On second thought
Does this life
Deserve me

Yadhira

Yes, she is such a marvelous being
Art so priceless she is to me
Damned is any man within her sight
How beautiful a smile so bright?
Intellect lost when she looks to me
Rather than speak I stutter abruptly
Although she already births a seed
For a man I can show him to her
Lost in her eyes I easily am
Oh, how I wish to be her man
Reality I live, she's not mine it seems
Even I get lost in dreams
So truly loved I wish her to be

My Prayer

What more can I lose
Besides life
What else can I give
That I haven't
Given twice
Take this life
And give me peace
Take this strife
And misery
Take this rain
And take this pain
Let all my losses
Be your gain
On my knees
I bow and pray

The Rose, Pt. 1

There's a story of a rose that grew with
peace, love, and hope, and because of a few
things he suffered and choked, replaced by
pain, hate, and hunger. He dreamed of a world
With pain no longer, as the rose grew he hid
his light and covered emotions with all his might
he loved the sun and admired the
moon. Each day and night his petals would
wither and then bloom and when time came
he grew tougher. He dropped his petals so
others may live

Alcohol

I take a sip
One to forget
Another sip
Cuz I love this shit
I grab the bottle and I just can't quit
A part of me it has become
To cover up shyness, hurt, and pain
It wasn't about fitting in
Just doing it once
I'd know I'd do it again
To cope with every thought of life
Knowing I did wrong when I should've did right
for years I spent trapped in juice
for years I've wanted, trying to hide the truth
I've put down the bottle of liquid sin
To cope with life through pad and pen
Part of me it once became
But I will end the cycle
Of my family's pain

The Rose, Pt. 2

Did you hear about the rose that grew from the crack in the forever?
Long live that rose that grew from the concrete when no else even
cared. Its colors withered and faded away, and hate replaced that which
was there. It taught itself the dangers of love to hide in the shadows of
increasing nature's law wrong, it learned to walk without fear, it mat-
tered not what others thought, the rose had all its necessities, so live
long, that lonely rose that lived without water and grew from the cracks
in the concrete.

Hurt

My only impatience is the coming of my demise
Because I've waited for love for so long
My heart has turned to ice
All pain is hidden
All grief is gone
How would you feel waiting for so long?
Things in life you won't understand
It was I turning away a helping hand
A helping hand
You who started all the pain
Who left me alone in pouring rain
Not that I, need someone to blame
I just know you'd do that shit again
Do I believe in love?
I can't say I do
But thanks again
It's all because of you

Wings

I know how I'm gonna die
I will look death straight in the eyes
I won't be scared, I will not cry
My spirit will live into the sky
I lived my life
Repaid my debts
Played my hand
Shuffled my deck
No one will mourn
No one will cry
Because peace will be with me
When I die
After crawling
I have learned to fly

Confused

Money is power and I don't have much
Love lasts forever but I don't have trust
It is wisdom that I seek
But not what I find
I clock in to work
Yet I'm lost in time
Love your family and friends
But love your enemy more?
Never be misused
How could I be
Why can't I see
That I'm so, so
Confused

Family Rules

We fuss, we fight
our house is filled with strife
Problems in life
We hold inside
Because talking
Just doesn't feel right
Our own blood we hate
No food on your plates
Then rent's due
But the money's low
it feels like
I'm in the world alone
I learned on a shoulder
But that too turned cold
but my love will always burn
A smile I'll always show
Cuz the sun is always out
Even when flowers
Refuse to grow
My doors are always open
My arms are stretched out wide
Because a family's love
Will never die

Shepherd

Every sheep
Needs a shepherd
Every shepherd
Need his sheep
Every son
Needs a father
Every father
Need his prodigal
Every paper needs a pen
Every pen
Needs a writer
But who am I to be
How will I shine
If my only home
Is the one in my mind

Looking Back

Before the past there was a beginning
Before the blessings there was sinning
Before trust there was lies
Before I live, will I die?
Before love there was hate
Before fortune there was fame
Before love there was lust
Before us
There was I
Before I smile I cry
Before me there was you
Before I knew it we were through

One Kiss

A kiss on the nose
Can make dreams come true?
It can bring the dead alive
Reverse curses too
A kiss on the cheek
Can cause the silent to speak
A kiss on the forehead
Makes one feel protection
A kiss down low
Can cause an erection
But a kiss on the lips
From the one you love
Will make one think, then thank
The man above

The Great Escape

What is it that's worse than love
It surely can't be hate
Because what has hurt the most
Is love that got away
I'm on a quest
To get it back
But oh, how my heart aches
Surely I will find
My love that got away

Home to Be

No matter what you do in this world alone
There's always a place for you to call home
Although I'm just a kid at heart
Reality struck at an early start
Didn't think I'd see that which I see
I didn't think that roses grew from concrete
So many thoughts flood my mind
I wanna love but don't have time
And misery loves company, this I know
But misery I will not show
And if you choose to live, live with love
Live and thank the man above
Cuz no matter what you do alone
There's always a place for you to call home

Dear Anita

I'm sorry you don't know who your father is
Sorry he's not man enough to raise his kids
And sorry I ever let you down
Cuz life is something we can't get around
Appreciate the little things
And know always you're a special queen
Never quit
But know the struggle
Win our battle and
You'll win another
Forgive your father
Forgive your mother
Forgive your sister
And your dear brother
Cuz loving you is what we do
Though never showed love
Is how we grow
Know one thing
You'll always rise
And the truth is always
in the eyes
I promise you
Bad times will come
And from these tests
You shall not run
Show respect and speak your mind.
And let them know
Your precious like time
Gain knowledge, wisdom, and understanding

And never turn
Your back on family
I pray to god, I'll see you grow
Cuz there's a part of me
You do not know
That part is love
I do not show
Although, I try to fight it
While needing it, I know
I try to hide it the best I can
While still trying
To be a man.
Its not the love that I fear
Its if the love is true and sincere
As soon as we met
It all returned
The love that as a child
I not wanted, but yearned
The love that from me
Was taken and lost,
The lost love, I pray
You never came across
Love your mother
Understand her mind
Understand her pain
Cuz they intertwine
Understand her heart
Understand her as a whole
For it was you,

Who brought back her glow
Show her you're there
And you'll never deceive her
Show her you love her
And you'll always need her
And for your sister
I'll take the blame
For not supporting her
Through all the pain
For telling her more than once
I didn't love her
Nor support her
As a brother
For turning my back
And not lending my shoulder
For not being her rock
Nor her soldier
Your sister loves you
And always will
Learn from her mistakes
Never hide what's real
And as for myself
I love you princess
I know this life
Is not the best
The crème de la crème,
Or the hidden treasure
Marked with an X
Search to see the pain in eyes

And realize, real eyes, see real lies
I pray you live a healthy life
Free of betrayal
Free of strife
To give you the world, is my dream
Cuz, the childhood years that I received
Are not the years, I want you to see
Keep your chest high
And never give up
Never let them take
Your pride and freedom
Never let them take your joy
Failure is not an option,
But yet a choice,
This is a letter for someone special
Who reminded me of love
When I was given worse
Reminded me of life
When I saw the hearse
This is a letter
For you and all you are
I'll never leave you
No matter how far
This life may take me
Or lead me through
One thing's for sure
I'll always love
You

Black Widow

They fear what's deeper than flesh
That which
They do not know
They fear the black widow
They fear the sun
They fear the stars
They fear what can end
Hunger and wars
They fear that they don't understand
This black widow
can heal true land
They fear the future
Because of the past
What's tougher than steel
but as fragile as glass
They fear each other
As one another
Sister, fear brother
Same goes
For father and mother
They fear that, that
Was never shared
But the black widow
Is always there
What is it
Who can it be
It's a bite from a spider
Of love, you see

The Land

Pain made me who I am
Surviving struggle made me a man
No one understands my pain
I just wanna see
The promised land

Imagine

I used to close my eyes
And always dream about heaven
Now I close my eyes
Then fall asleep around eleven
Now I live to live
Give to give
And death is what I seek
I never cheat nor steal
and the truth is what I speak
It's always sunny where?
Can you please show me?
So I'll never go
Cuz my life's greatest lessons
Have come through
Sleet, hail, and snow

To Be Different

They're not gonna like me
Vow the words that I speak
They're not gonna like me
Cuz their minds are weak
Yes, she's beautiful
But what's her soul like
is she true in the dark
As well as in the light
He's powerful as well
While he doesn't do right
He just needs love
She just needs might
They're not gonna like her
Because of her mind
They're not gonna like her
Cuz she precious like time

True Dreams

I wanna tell her
Her dreams come true
I wanna whisper
that which
She never knew
I wanna feel
Her immaculate touch
Fulfill every dream
And every loss
I wanna smell
Her every fragrance
Shower her with diamonds
And remarkable banquets
I wanna taste
Her every anchor
Every kiss
In every flavor
I wanna hear
Her every voice
And in her name
I will rejoice
I wanna see
Her alluring smile
Be a part of her journey
Every step and mile
But these things, to me
Are just a dream

A dream
That's never new
But at night I pray to God
That all dreams come true

What If

The greatest minds have the greatest addictions
What if my mind isn't so great?
I just refuse to listen
The greatest successors
Have the most pain
What if I haven't been through enough
And success isn't my aim
Even when I win
What if I lose
What if every lie I told
Turned out to be true
So many things in the world
I can turn out to be
What if
All I wanna be is me

The Pen or Sword

On this pad
I simply write
It's my strength
My hidden might
Through every struggle
And every strife
Every drop of ink
Used at night
on this pad
I tell no lie
No running from the truth
on this pad I am a person
Known by just a few
On this pad I show a talent
Hidden by a guard
So you tell me what's sharper
The pen or the sword

Trapped

I'm trapped
In a world I don't fit in
I'm trapped by
Days and lots of gin
I'm trapped
Thinking someone or thing could save me
Trapped inside these walls
And it's driving me crazy
I'm trapped
But in front of people
I do not show
Whatever's holding me hostage
Could you let me go?
Because trapped
I wanna be no longer
Please let go, my mind, body, and soul
Because freedom
Is my only hunger

To Mom

Mama, it's hard for me to cry
Sometimes in the shower
I force tears out my eyes
Sometimes on my knees
I ask God why
Mama, it's hard for me to cry
We got kids killing kids
And nobody wants to strive
Nobody's teaching the young
So where will their minds fly
Everybody's a little racist still
I see fear behind their eyes
No truth from their mouth, it's just their lies
It's all darkness, no light
It's all wrong and not right
Mama, it's hard for me to cry
There's sex but no love
Closure but no hugs
Everyone wants to make moves
But haters all scare to budge
Blood on the floor
Stains scattered from drugs
Mama, it's hard for me to cry
I stare in your face
As you see right through me
Having to be a man
For as a child you never knew me
But as tears leave your face
Let the sky provide thunder

Cuz, I sit and watch as you cry
While in my mind I wonder,
Why,
Mama, is it hard for me to cry

So Alone

I remember looking over the fence
At the children's home
Looking for a place
To call my own
Looking for a place
To finally call home
I remember when I had a family
But still felt so alone
I remember when I didn't have a dollar
But still denied every loan
I remember when I felt pain
But would not let out a moan
remember show and tell
When I had nothing to own
I remember a lot of things
But will never forget
Being alone

WWYD

All I ask for in life
Is pen and some paper
family and friends are here now
But they'll leave me later
If I asked for a drink
Would you share your water?
Or would you watch my life dry
As I fight this hunger
If I asked for a hand
Would you help pick me up
Or would you leave me in sand
Fighting while stuck
Would you chase a dollar?
While watching me beg
Or try to become life in my lungs
If you thought, I was dead
Treat me the way I treat you
Cuz all that you ask
Is for someone that's true
And will that I ask
Is that you keep my sky blue

To Duprice

Every day I miss her
She's a part of me, I know
But I never would've thought
Our hearts would be fearful to grow
Every day I hate her
No, I don't
I take it back
Every day I hate
The childhood we had
But not to throw no pity
Strongminded, yes, we are
Our time in life is too short
But there is life beyond the starts
In this world that we're given
We are never told the truth
And the only lie I said
Was I've never loved you
You are my heart
Oh, well, there's more
Anita, taniya, joi
Surely can't forget
Every other sister and boy,
Love Devlynn

Mirror

What makes you laugh
What makes you smile
What makes you enjoy life?
For a while
What brings you pain
What brings you sanity
What makes you feel love
What makes a family
What brings your health
What makes your wealth
What made you write
A letter to yourself
Was is it the same thing
That makes you
Wanna kill yourself
Was it the same hate and love you felt?
What is it
What can it be
All these questions
The mirror asked me

Heaven Sent

If I don't make it into heaven
Can I at least peek through the clouds
Can I stare astonished at the gates?
While in my thoughts, thinking wow
If I don't make it into heaven
Can I smell an angel's scent?
May I touch a halo
And see blessings
Forever Heaven sent
If I don't walk the street of gold
Can I at least take a picture
And keep it in my pocket
If the signs say
Can't take it with you
If I don't make it into heaven
Last but not least
Can I sit at the table
Feeding my stomach with a feast
Before I melt in hell
And burn along with the beast
If I don't make it into heaven
On earth can I at least see it

Story of 12

Twelve people who became soldiers
Twelve soldiers who became bold
In our hands
Our lives we now hold
Our minds now pure
Our hearts no longer cold
Different walks of life
All together for one goal
And there's nothing in life we shall regret
Because life
We haven't finished yet
Seeking to heal pain
In the bottom of a glass
Running away from things in our past
A brighter future we keep our eyes on
A higher power we now can lean on
And shall we ever fall short and forget
The journey's just begun
We haven't finished yet

They Say

They say let go of the past
But the past hurts
I've heard stories of diamonds coming
From this earthly dirt
There's something about love
That I don't like
The way it passes these days
 I'm like why try
They say don't judge and always pray
But even answers don't come this way
They say they're there
And how I've always needed them
Something about their line
I once never reached them
They say stay true
But their lies
Come easy
If I stood behind glass
Would they see the real me?
Even a judge
Can be unruly
If I gave you my time again
Would you still use me?
If a fool, fools a fool
Only a wise man can fool me

Tell Me the Truth

Tell me I got potential
Tell me that I'm a writer
Tell me that when I speak words in your ear
It sets your soul on fire
Tell me that I'm special
Tell me that you'll please me
That you love me and will always need me
Tell me that I'm real
Tell me that I'm true
Tell me why the only one I ever loved is you
Tell me that you love me
Tell me that you need me
Tell me the truth
That you'll never leave me
Tell me that I'm goofy
That I make you wild
Tell me I took away your pain
Replaced it with a smile
Tell me I'm special
Tell me I'm loved
Tell me I'm an angel
Sent from above
Tell me your problems
Tell me your pain
Tell me my presence
Took them away
But most of all
Tell me the truth
Of course, you'll leave
But tell me love is true

Misunderstood

He was scared to lose her
Cuz he fell in love
He was scared to lose her
Cuz all she was
More beauty than life
More power than death
Presented herself prestigious
And nothing less
he was fire
Raised from pain
Thinking love was just a game
In his life she walked
And he changed
But due to pain
he was scared to ever
Love again
He held back love
With all his might
With distance now between tempers
Of course she lost the fight
He was scared to lose her
Cuz all she was
When he lost her, it was due,
Cuz he was scared to love

Out of Mind

Over my life
I have no sovereignty
People like me
We rose from poverty
We come from dirt
Rose from the gutter
Rest so much pain
And nothing other
Yes I cheat and yes I steal
For the one I love
Will I kill?
I pray this life will bring me peace
I'm tired of misery
Tired of grief
I'm tired of pain
Tired of tears
so yet,
I leave this here
I hope God sees my heart in pure
If heaven's just another door
Still I rise
And I've risen some more

The Kid

There's a beast in me I thought I tamed
A beast in me without a name
There's a heart in me I thought I hid
A heart in me I lost as a kid
There's a smile in me I do not show
A smile in me that lost its glow
There's a joke in me I do not tell
 A joke in me with a story to yell
There a writer in me without a pen
A writer in me lost in sin
There's a man in me that sees the truth
A man in me with nothing to lose
There a beast in me I thought I tamed
 A beast in me and I hid his pain

Passion & Pain

Passion and pain
Brings sun after rain
Cuz passion is sun
And rain is pain
What strives us to do more
When we were given less than
The answer is simple
It's simply passion
From a dark night
And a cloudy day
Passion suddenly
Took pain away
And when pain returned
When rain
Attempted to sweep the sun away
We thought to ourselves
What a cloudy day
But in this way
Be not dismayed
Again passion
Took
Pain away

My Mind

I'm from a place where they sell dope
and have rap dreams
Do anything
To see the color green
Pockets starved sometimes but Mama made sure
We'd always eat
Daddy made sure a pair of shoes were on our little feet
and love we promised
We'd always keep
I'm from a place where hills are steep
And valleys low
A place in the dark
Where the shadows grow
A place I'd advise you
Not to go
I'm from a place where flowers
Don't grow
And in the end
When the lights go off
When we've lived our life
Whether a win or loss
We'll never forget the little place
Always in our hearts
We come across

If I Die Tonight

If I die tonight
Make sure my casket is tight
So my soul doesn't leap out
On the wrong boat or flight
And if I die tonight
See if I lived right
Through pain and strife
I lived my life
If I die tonight
Make sure my wings are ready
Cuz I've taken on Earth
And I'm taking on heaven
If I die tonight
Tell them what I did
Tell them how I struggled
Remained humble
And lived

To Endure

Never turn your back on the ones you trust
Never fall in love with the ones you lust
For if you do you will be lost
Betrayed and scarred
By the ones you crossed
Money is good, yes
But what about freedom
If a village raises a child
What comes from a kingdom?
Pleasure my flesh
And endear my mind
Treasure my chest
Waste not my time
These are the words I share with you
Speak knowledge from your mouth
Let us all be true
On your feet
Stand tall and strong
Defending what's right
Against all wrongs
All answers
Come from the heart
And sometimes the end
is the needed start

Her Ballet

Her moves are as beautiful as a Grand Jeté
But as I speak she turns away
Her body moves just like the ocean sways
Every motion she makes is like a Croisé
The way she performs with ever Plié
I pray she'll never stop as she dances my way
She walked in my life smooth as an ensemble
The way she put on the way she sweats
Then she shows off her Pirouette
There's no words to describe her, she's just the best
How tight her legs, how rotund her breast
She suddenly performs the move arabesque
But once again life is not fair
In the opposite direction she dances on air
In the opposite direction Tour En L'air
With every stroke, with every play
I fell in love with her ballet

Finish Line

This plant is my food
This liquor is my water
Because in this world
I chose not to be sober
Or at least I thought
With my last dollar
Drags I bought
I cried at night
Because life I lost
I know there's hope
I know there's life
I know on this path
There will be light

The Doctor

I told the doctor
That pain doesn't go away
That happiness is an illusion
That always comes my way
I told the doctor
That love has long been lost, man
That we would rather appreciate money
Than what's more important
You see
I told the doctor
That friends make the best enemies
That time is what I am
Or what I seek to be
I told the doctor
That I'm blinded by my ways
But the doctor didn't listen
he looked at me with craze

Wages of Sin

If the wages of sin
is death
And in the end
There's nothing left
Mark a cross upon my chest
Let me breathe my final breath
If the wages of sin are death
Let's live a better life
Forgive me once
Forgive me twice
Speak to me of my wrongs and rights
If the wages of sin are death
Let me write my wrongs in pen
Allow me to prove my innocence
And if I close this wrong again
Forgive me, Father
For I have sinned
If the wages of sin are death

Two Things

2 things you can do
Earn respect
Or act a fool
But you can't do both
2 things you can do
But yet you have to choose
See, this life
Gave me misery
Happiness or pain
Which will remain
If you are for me
Then why use me
I loved you once
I love you forever
But you tried me once
Not thinking I'm clever

Love Me

Love is a jump so beautifully made
A leap in the air, like a Grand Jeté
Love is a drug made
Not to be used but shared
It's the only thing in this world
So precious that's feared
Love is a book
Never fully read
Important to our body
Like water and bread
It is a labyrinth
In which we get lost
Love is a jewel
That we stumble across
It is a fire
Feeling wonderful when burned
Love is what
My mind, body, and soul
Forever yearn

Faith

I know loss
I know rain
I know suffering
I know pain
I know tears
I know fear
I know one thing
It'll disappear

Mirror Pt. 2

It shows us who we are
But will never tell us
Reflecting a pure image
Of something zealous
In the midst of those
Who's hearts are jealous
Staring back in our own eyes
Is someone fearless
WE always stare
But never know
The person staring back
And the paths he'll go
We can clean, we can wipe
But can't make the past go away
What is it about this mirror
And the man
Staring back at my face
What is it
About the potential
In the reflection
That's gone to waste

My Quest

Destiny told me this was destined
 Love told me she's lost
Faith told me keep going
And
Hope told me don't stop
Age doesn't define life
Only years
Pain doesn't bring a smile
Only tears
This life is a scary sight
Sometimes I look up to God
Tell him I'm coming
But it's gonna be a scary flight
It's not death
One must overcome
It's life
Time is for eternity
So it's never too late
In a world full of demons
Angels despise hate

Seeds

I want a kid one day
So I can teach them how to play
Teach them
How to make it
In this world
And pass the sky
They way we're living now
We serve to perish
Cuz life we took for granted
And we did not cherish

Why

Why be the test subject
When you can be the final exam
Why be with a thousand
When you can have your own man
Why lose what you have
While searching for someone new
Why start a new life?
When the old one's not through

The Warning

By the time I had my support
It was too late
By the time I was fed
I didn't have a plate
By the time I know
Of course I was lost
By the time they forgot
Was the time I taught
If love exists
Then it must be true
The rose
From the concrete
That finally grew
And once it grew
It would never die
And they hate this rose
I wonder why
Through every loss
The rose would win
Past all the drugs
And pods of gin
No matter what
This rose would give
To watch his people
Flourish and live
No matter what
It rose on top
Beware this rose
You come across

And learn
Every lesson
From
Every loss

As a Man

As a man
Can I bring a smile to your face?
As a man in you
Can I place my faith?
Like snow in the desert
Come melt in these hands
Like a king and his queen
Give me this dance
Like coals in a fire
Burn me with your love
Cuz like a child and his toys
I could never have enough
Finish me
When I'm incomplete
Be my words
 When I fail to speak
My every strength
When I'm feeling weak
Like a winter's blanket
Cover me
But don't you ever
Stop loving me

Music

When I'm down and low
Or even in the clouds
Lost in this world
And can't find my way out
There's people that speak
Their voice over a beat
Starting a fire in my soul
That moves down to my feet
Kendrick taught me to fight
With words stronger than a missile
Michael holds a note
Lasting longer than any whistle
Biggie mastered Juicy
Z-ro still making hits
Pac taught me how to talk to females
Woman or a bitch
Kanye dropped the ball
Chance picked it up
Cole earned his respect
Big Sean and Wale
Don't have enough
So if you feel like giving up
Or you wanna be alone
Listen to Bob Marley
Let music satisfy your soul

To Joi (Someday)

Some days I go not thinking about you
Some days I go thinking love is not true
Some days I go and do feel weak
Cuz someday I go thinking
Emotion I can't speak
Some days I go wondering how you've been
Some days I spend lost in the wind
Some days I pray that you'll find wealth
Some days I pray that we'll all find ourselves
Some days I know you sit and wonder why
Some days I know you sit alone and cry
Some days I see a happy you that smiles
Some days I see it hidden for a while
Some days I ask why you couldn't have a father
Some days I ask why I could have a mother
Someday I wonder will we ever see each other
Every day I wonder will I ever be a brother

Within Me

I got the spirit
That people like
Am I wrong
Or am I right
I got the spirit
That wants to be free
Through this pad and pen
Can't you see
Raised by friends and family
Raised by friends of enemies
Raise my hand and call me king
A mamba mentality
I have in me
A king
In a peasant's clothes
Grab my ring and grasp my robe
Listen
To stories untold
Untold stories told by me
Listen and watch my soul
Be free

My Question

I pray for my enemies
I pray for their wealth
I pray for my mother
And her mental health
I pray for my friends
I pray for their families
I pray that my sisters
Will see the man in me
I pray through arid times
I pray through good
I pray for the suburbs
Along with the hood
I pray for all
No matter why, what, or who
But most of all
Does anyone pray for me, too?

Meant to Be

If the truth is meant to be said
Then what's all this truth
Inside my head
If lies were meant to be told
Why is it that lies get old
A quest for wisdom
And understanding
 A question for love
In search of family
one question asked
No answers told
With only applied knowledge
Can man grow old
A sober mind
Was once a goal
But instead of truth
Lies were told
And if the truth
Should not be shared
Then curse my lips
'Cause the truth lives here

Thanks

Fuck dying broke
I don't wanna die alone
I pray to God for the good times
As well as a happy home
I pray to God they smile
That I may raise a child
That the fact I'm broke now
Won't last but a while
I thank God for bad times
Along with the lessons
I thank God for the curse
Along with the blessings

Remember Me By

Knowledge, laughter, and power
Weed and liquor on the hour
Knowledge, laughter, power
Is this really how we live
How much does a dollar cost?
If you knew
Would you still give?
Knowledge, laugher, power
Each a steering within these words
oven the highest mountain
Lowest villages
I made it through these worlds
A rusted spoon
An empty bowl
I ate among the less
 with rusted spoon
And empty bowl
I ate among the best
Knowledge, laughter, power
Because ignorance is bliss

Water

Words are like water
They trickle in your ear
The softest words up close
Saying what we want to hear
Words are like water
They can freeze us in our tracks
Saying the wrong words
Is like falling on your back
Because water turns to ice
And when not frozen
Slipping when wet
So be careful with what you say
Speak with no regret
Words are like water
Flowing east with the river
But do not fight the current
Nor let them see you shiver
Words are like water
Choose wisely how you pour
And when there's
Word on the street
Simply shut the door

Purusha

They see the gift
That I don't see
but don't see the past
And history
They see the pain
I do not show
But don't know
The roots
From where I grow
They smell the smell of victory
But in me
They smell defeat
They taste the taste
Of every fall
But don't pass my taste
Big or small
They hear the call of every phone
But when I call
I stand alone
They feel the feel
Of every touch
But when I touch
They've had enough
So here I stand I stand alone
Here I stand
Because I've grown

Existence

Being alone makes you strong
Being alone makes you suffer
Yeah, it's hard sometimes
But being alone make you tougher
Being alone brings clouds
Being alone brings thunder
Yeah, it brings the storm
But being alone makes you wonder
Being alone shows you love
Being alone brings understanding
Yeah, it's hard to love
But being alone shows your family
Being alone brings wisdom
Being alone brings pain
Yeah, it brings wonders of death
But being alone shows life
And all that we can gain

Done

I'm done
Done with it all
Done climbing ladders
Just to feel the fall
I'm done
Done with the storms
Done with the people
Who never made me warm
I'm done
Done with the styles
Done with society
And all the fake smiles
I'm done
Done with the wind
And all the rain
So now that I'm done
I drop my pen
I turn the page

To the Wealthy

If you take away war
You've taken away currency
if you take away money
You've taken away power
Am I right or am I wrong
How can freedom sing
Without a song
If you take away knowledge
You take away hope
If you take away love
Only hate and pain can elope
You take away more
To give me the least
So if you try to take more
I will make war
And bring you peace

Never, Never Say

Never say
You don't deserve
Mistakes are lessons
 That we've earned
Never bring guilt
Upon yourself
For you will only hold back
Your health and wealth
The meek shall inherit the earth
Yes
The wise come up from beneath the dirt
Blessed
Those who learn through their life
Doing bad while trying right
Never hate your wrong and mistakes
From these places
Knowledge we make

Drunk

One more drink
One more thought
One more fight
One more loss
One more drink
One bliss more
One more hit
One more kiss
Sip some more
One more miss
Fix more one
One more drink
Another bottle
please
One more drink
More, more wish
Wish more sip
One more thing
I'm drunk

Making Love

Have you ever
Ever used ice on a drunk night
Ever been choked and fucked right
Ever been smacked and bit
Around ear
Whispered and liked
Put your lip upon mine
My lips lust your legs
Later twined
Ever been touched with the softest love
Ever make love with the hardest touch
Ever had cum run down your thighs
Ever been turned around
Or cherished like wine
Have you ever ridden a man
Like a wild horse
Or fell off the bed
Like an obstacle course
Ever been dropped
Then picked up
I know you've been fucked
But have you made love

Is Coming

What's that smell?
That takes your breath
Takes all the air
Up out your chest
What's that stench?
When nothing's left
I finally understand
I loved my life
That smell of death

Real Riches

I don't want riches like Mansa Musa
Though I was born a slave
But not like Kunta
A slave to society
And my people's debt
Like Jesus in the garden
There nights I've wept
I don't want fame
Like any celebrity
I want life
Along with liberty
Don't tell me lies
Because the truth hurts
For I will be an honest man
While I walk this earth
I don't want fortune
Nor any kingdom
I search for knowledge
I search for wisdom

Queen

If I treated, you like a Queen
Would you see the King in me?
If I asked what dreams are possible
Would your answer be everything
If I only had a dollar
Would you still love me
If I gave you all I had
Would that even be enough
If I lacked respect, honor, and ambition
Maybe that would catch attention
Call you a bitch
Instead of the woman you are
Then maybe you would listen
If I had the truth
And fed you lies
You would eat them all
If I walked a thousand miles
Just to see you
Would you then answer my call
So many things I truly doubt
I'm sure that you can see
But that's the cause in this world
They've surely doubted me

My Brother

He packed a pistol and blunt
Before he hit the road
Dropped some advice
Supplied laughter
Memories and dreams
We shared and told
He popped some pills
Smoke a blunt and
Would even have a drink
Conversing with him
He would make you sit, laugh, and think
And these one more
That wonders out
No one knows what he's about
he loved his liquor
Shared his need
Chasing many dreams
There's a story of
Three ghetto musketeers
That'll go down in history
A group known by a few
That turned from friends to family

Love of a Woman

I miss the remorse in a woman's eyes
The taste between a woman's thighs
The touch of love and peace she brings
 With a gentle look a woman alone
Can calm a pack of hungry lions
And any beast she sees
Oh, so silent, but could silence a crowd
the way a woman can stand
So elegant, robust
Prestige and proud
The way she cooks
And woman, oh so special, what a treat
The way a woman tastes
So soft, tender
Valuable and sweet
The way she bears a man's every pain
With her own strength she lifts the man
To rise up once again
I miss the name "woman"
In a world full of bad bitches and shit
I miss the definition of a woman
It gets no simpler
No simpler than this

Dear America

America, I'm just a man
Without a dollar, just a dream
America, I'm just a man
And from me you've taken everything
America, I'm just a man
Why do I have to be a nigger?
You've traded in your known tied ropes
Replaced them with badges and triggers
You traded in the truth
Fed me twisted muop;lite lies
America, I'm just a man
Just an ordinary guy
I just want to prosper
See my people finally succeed
But America, you had a plan
When you set my people free
America, I'm just a man
Trying to escape post slavery
America, I'm just a man
That you fear
Because you did not make me
For I am just a man
Have you noticed lately,
America?

Intimate

I stared at her beauty for hours
But as time passed I realized it was only seconds
Here I am before her fully clothes,
But my soul, naked

The Pear

If I was a fruit
A little tainted or bruised
Would you still pay your dollar, to partake of my juice?
If I was a man
Who lost all his wealth
His greatest treasures, mind and wealth
Would you stay with me?
As this valley we cross
And become greater, than any treasure I've lost
Had I been a seed lost in the wind
Would you grab me, plant me, and help me grow?
Or like other strong trees
Just watch me blow
No, you don't love me
It's easier for you, just to say so

Caged Bird

Even when all I wanted to do was talk.
Not even a female would listen.
Unless I was going inside them.
I remember a time I'd be in a room
Crack a joke and everyone would laugh
Oh, how funny it is
They forgot about my ass
A few months down turned me into a memory
Lord, I swear when I'm free
They gonna remember me
When these broken wings fly
Treat me how you did when I was caged
Words from a solitary mind
A man that's caged

When You Love

When you love somebody
You miss them
You miss them when they look away from you for a quick second
Wondering what could have distracted them from your beauty
When you love somebody
You kiss them
You kiss them like it's the last second on earth and life will last as long
as your lips touch
You hold them
Hold them close and tight so no evil or discrepancy can come be-
tween you
When you love somebody you choose to stay
You stay because to be away from them would hurt you more than
anything in this world
But then I ask
Do you love somebody?

To Fall

There's a reason we "fall" in love
If we were to "trip"
We would have a chance to catch ourselves
And we would stop,
Stop ourselves from knowing if its hurts
You see when you love somebody sometimes it's going to hurt
But just like when you fall
You get back up and look forward
But how would we know what getting up feels like if we were just to "trip"
When you love somebody
You find all the reasons to fall
And not just "trip"
It's easy to catch somebody while they're tripping
But who forgets the ones who helped them when they fell
To fall in love

Lay

Lay on top of me
Tell me your dreams
Fear not vulnerability
Tell me your scheme
Suppress the evil spirit
And open your eyes
Realize the debt
Of becoming alive
Hold back no pain
Erupt with pleasure
Release the weight of the world
Off your shoulders
Come fly with me
At last, spread your feathers
Lay on top of me
Tell me your dreams
At a time when I had nothing
You made me king
So come, come lay with me

Sex

Close your eyes, take a trip with me
Nonetheless, pure ecstasy
When you're next to me
Receiving nothing
But the best of me
Take a ride, relax and then rest
Wake up, let's communicate
About, what's next

Drinking

Drinking, thinking, smoking thoughts of why mama wasn't there
She gave birth but not love
Why Mama and Daddy didn't care
Why do I hurt the ones I love?
The ones I love don't love me back
But the ones who love me
Were never there
This the answer to many questions
On why life isn't fair
I was drinking, thinking, smoking
And not giving life a care
I made it out the gutter
Without a mother, sister, brother
So what I'm doing, drinking, smoking, thinking
I never needed one another
I'm sorry, this anger gets me
Sometimes I lose control
Cuz I did it on my own
Drink, smoke, think, drink, think, drink, smoke
Pour the drink, sit back and think
On this life I never choose
Where's the answer

Words

Copulation, fornication, procreation
With hesitation, without relation
Lust
No hesitation, intimate relations, no replace, breathtaking
Love
Fly away, to a higher place, no trace of space, pure beauty and grace
Live
Relax and smile, just for a while
Joke and play, enjoy the day
Laugh
Turn your ear, applaud and cheer
Learn to speak, when your mind's not weak
Listen

Reversed

I know how it feels, false hope,
But who am I to blame
Pains the bullet
You held the rifle
I was at the far end of the range
I done did so much wrong
It's only right, wrong done to me
With every letter
On this paper,
I allow my pen to bleed
I know how it is to cry
To bury, lose and grief
I've been there, paid a price to win
This debt is far from cheap
I know how it is to change
You stayed left, I went right
I know the feeling to remember
So I pray for you at night

The Comparison

The crazy thing about love
It's kind of like death
You know it's there
But never know when
It will take your breath
Away from you,
And out of your chest
Your soul will rise
But what will be left
Death and lost love
It's hard to accept
The crazy thing about death
It's kind of like love
When it happens you'll never be ready
Just make sure you play it steady
One will cry and feel lost at time
You see, love and death will make you lose your mind
Every person will experience both
Make smart choices
Know who you are
Embrace death at times
And when love comes
Let her know she shines
Because death will take her
Or take you first
But there's no love
Once you leave this earth
You see, love and death are the same to be
Because both have history

Both can cause misery
And there will be
No love left
If your love leaves
You will just sit
And wait for death

Magnificent

She's so beautiful
Somebody had to paint her
A beast so wild
I didn't have to tame her
Cuz she knew game
And she held anger
She had hunger in her stomach
And fire in her heart
It's torch scorching hot
From the very start
For she knew it was love
That her body yearned
And like I said,
Love, she faintly learned
Eyes so true
You can see yourself
Her body richer
Than anyone's wealth
But like a ship in a crazed sea
Her gaze I have lost,
Like a man stranded on an island
Her praise I pray,
I came back across

3 Wishes

If I had three wishes
I'd probably wish for 1000 more wishes
Things that would not only bring me riches
I'd wish for anything that could make me feel good
And wish away morning wood
A wish to make people smile
Possibly one, that takes away taxes for a little while
I wouldn't wish to be a leader
Until I wish to be a public speaker
I'd wish away all hunger and war
A wish for a 5-star place
To feed the poor
I'd wish for a woman, with the body of a goddess
A wish for a queen, who's quiet and modest
I'd wish that our skies are always blue
Or maybe just wish
For others wishes to become true

Two Freaks

There's this thing stuck in my sheets
In my sheets, two, two-legged freaks
It's not one that small and creeps
It's the people wetting the sheets
As she rides with passion so deep
My body buckles, I'm suddenly weak
I pull and lick, grip and bite
These are freaks, who love the night
There's all eight limbs which are intertwined
Her anatomy pressed, tangled with mine
Their bodies flow, moving so smooth
Imagine an ocean current, made of wine
Whose age has only, mastered its taste
This is passion not put to waste
There's a freak who moans, then screams
Dreams do come true
For she was once a dream
There's a freak, whose liquids are sweet
Being trapped in a web is a marvelous treat
Her eyes so dark, but tell the truth
Her venomous poison is a delightful juice
Divine are her hips and her hips perhaps
Me in her, her in my sheets
It's like a trap
For a freak, I too turn out to be
Me in her
And her on me
There's a fire burning internally
A fire that will burn
For eternity

Unspoken Words

Unspoken words of
unheard-of thoughts
Love shall be found
Peace won't be lost
Unspoken words of
unheard-of thoughts

Jasmyne's Poem

A bird sat next to me and asked
If I was scared
I said I was not
And asked why he cared
He asked, "If I was in danger, would you protect me?"
I said, "I would try."
"How?" he demanded, now perched on the tree.
"Well," I announced, "it depends on the situation you're in, these
questions make me uncomfortable, I can't pretend."
"But why?" he sung. "Your answers are true
and for what I commend you."
I replied, "You have wings so you can fly,
why do you need the help of mine?"
"You're right," he whispered, "and that's the key,
I am fine and perfectly free."
"So why are you scared?" he asked of me.
"Your wings extend quite beautifully," he continued to speak.
"Fear is what held you down, I do believe."
I was bewildered and beside myself
For I felt too inadequate to think high of myself
Yet, I have great power inside myself
I knew he was right in spite of myself
I dropped to my knees and cried to myself
For I was too blind to see
All that I had become to be
and the only thing holding me back was me
I was scared